Search Engine Optimization

A Complete Guide on Everything You Need to Know about SEO

KENNETH LEWIS

ISBN:1518796540
ISBN-13: 978-1518796548

DEDICATED TO
THE READER

May you achieve success in all your
business and entrepreneurial endeavors.

TABLE OF CONTENTS

INTRODUCTION

Search engine optimization (SEO) is the internet art of making a particular website or webpage appear higher on the results of a search engine list. Almost every internet user in the 21st century finds the majority of content they wish to view through websites such as Google or Yahoo. Whether people are looking for an answer to some pointless trivia they don't know or whether people are actively looking for products to buy, search engines are the tool for the job.

However, it is not enough for a website or webpage to be listed on a popular search engine like Google. If a website isn't located on the first page of results, or even the first two or three entries, chances are the majority of searchers are not going to look at that webpage.

If people are not looking at a particular webpage then the purpose of that webpage, such as advertising or product sales, will not be fulfilled. Ultimately, getting a webpage to appear as the first, second or third result on a popular search engine results in a massive difference in the amount of internet traffic they receive and corresponding purchases.

With this in mind, any business that uses the internet to attract customers or sell products *needs* to be familiar with search engine optimization. Search engine optimization is simply too vital to ignore.

Yet search engine optimization is far from simple. It is a multi-faceted, complicated concept that requires intelligent manipulation and research of several corners of the internet.

To master SEO, you need to produce quality content or other attractive goods to generate initial interest. You need to systematically and continuously increase the amount of links and references to this content via blogs, social media and other sympathetic websites.

It is also of utmost importance to know your audience and consumer better then you know yourself. If someone is looking to find a product or service online, you need to be intimately familiar with what words or phrases that person will enter in the search bar. It is of no use being the highest result for a search entry that no-one is entering. Researching and understanding what keywords people use when looking for your product or market area will increase the likelihood of people finding your content.

You also need to tactfully and skillfully embed these keywords in your website or webpage content in intelligent ways, resulting in a greater chance that a search engine will match search entries to your webpage. Conversely, introducing irrelevant or misguided keywords in your text will confuse and bewilder the search engines, attracting the wrong consumers and audiences. Moreover, simply spamming keywords within your text will reduce the quality of content, lowering your audience retention.

All these before mentioned factors barely scratch the surface of search engine optimization. Learning how to exploit social media for your own ends is another crucial skill; you need to be effective and efficient in getting social media users to share and forward the content you produce for free advertising and greater connectivity.

To further pile on the complexity, your website or webpage needs to be attractive and original in design. Global companies such as Apple and Samsung have mastered simple, zen-inspired layouts that retain the attention of internet goers through carefully crafted aesthetics.

Even more importantly, search engines use a variety of markers, calculations and numerous other factors in their algorithms to determine which website finishes first in the SEO race. Understanding the official and formal purposes of meta-tags, headers, spiders robots, paragraphs and cannon descriptions in your website page HTML will give you the insight to convince the search engines you are the best result they can find.

Another factor to take in to consideration are third-party websites and auxiliary resources. These tools can provide you with various data and statistics to make all the previously mentioned SEO techniques more accurate and informed. They will provide you with a wealth of useful information such as the exact level of user retention for your website or the conversion rate from website views to product purchases. All of these numbers and charts can help you distill and refine your SEO practices until your techniques are well-polished and your SEO success is inevitable.

Finally, you need to be aware, at least to some extent, of what *not to do*. The more you learn about SEO techniques and the greater level of insight you gain, the greater the temptation to shortcut the system can be; to attempt to cheat and abuse the tendencies of the search engines for your own gain.

Let it be made clear; there is nothing saintly or innocent about SEO; all SEO techniques and attempts are for the purpose of profit or some other marketing feature. Nonetheless, certain techniques and certain actions are considered unfair or especially exploitative and will not be tolerated by the search engines you rely upon. Search engines are becoming smarter and the methods they use to find websites are increasingly refined.

If a search engine recognizes that you are using a lazy or dishonest measure to increase your SEO, it may deliberately ignore that content or punish your website by placing it further down the search engine results. If you go too far, your website or ISP can be blacklisted, ensuring that it will not appear on a search engine again. To avoid these sorts of results requires an understanding of what lines not to cross and the insidious techniques that lead you into dangerous waters.

All of this required learning may seem overwhelming at initial glance. Fortunately, this book will break down all these techniques into bite-size digestive instruction and methodology. After reading *SEO 2016* you will learn everything you need to know to improve your internet presence and business' success through wise and effective SEO management.

Finally, take your business or product to the new level by learning ways in which you can use Facebook to maximize your marketing efforts in the sneak preview of 'Facebook Marketing: How to Use Facebook for Effective Internet Marketing and Social Media

Success'.

1

SEARCH ENGINE OPTIMIZATION BASICS

The nature of search engine optimization was briefly touched upon in the introduction; SEO is the method internet marketers use to increase how high their website or webpage is presented on the results of a search engine query. This chapter will expand on some of the foundational aspects of SEO and the prerequisite terminology necessary to gain a thorough understanding of this complex topic.

Search Engines

To start with, let us briefly talk about search engines. Search engines are websites that use specialized software to filter and search through the World Wide Web to produce particular results. Search engines can be features on particular websites, such as the search engine people use on Facebook to find particular content or other existing users. Alternatively, search engines can be their own entity and the predominant feature of a website or company, such as the search engine provided by Google.

Search engines can provide a variety of results. For example, some search engines are specialized for professional and academic purposes and will only provide links to scientific papers or content published within a certain journal or respected magazine (such as the Web of Knowledge search engine).

Other search engines are more generalized, returning results that match the entered content in any conceivable way. Google for example provides website links, related advertisements, images, relevant news articles, videos and several other categories. Content can be filtered by users so that only the type of desired content appears.

Search engine optimization is an internet marketing strategy that exploits search engines. Search engine optimization aims to understand how search engines work and what search engine users are entering in order to reach certain audiences more effectively. By knowing these factors, SEO allows marketers to ensure that their website or webpage is within the first couple of results from a search engine query and thus receives the greatest amount of internet traffic possible.

Each search engine uses its own software to decide what result is best suited to the search query. However, despite individual differences for particular search engines, the basics of how each search engine works follows generic rules.

The True Complexity of the Internet

Before exploring these rules however, it is important to have a little insight into how the internet actually works. For most of us, we tend to treat the internet how we treat cars or complicated electrical products; a black box of inputs and outputs. Strictly speaking we know what a car does; it is a machine that we can drive to get from A to B.

Yet at some point in time, it became the consensus opinion that we do not need to understand how a car works. If you ask people how an engine functions or what pieces of gear are under the car hood, the overwhelming majority of people do not know.

The same is true for the internet. People talk about the World Wide Web but the understanding of this term is vague and loose. This poor understanding is serviceable for the rest of the population, but as an internet marketer and SEO enthusiast you need to enter the matrix and go deeper.

The World Wide Web is a collection of documents stored on a server accessed by an internet connection. Every website you encounter is a document written in a programming code called HTML. In the same way you might have a Microsoft word file, PowerPoint or Excel document, a website is basically also just a document or a series of documents that are interconnected.

HTML and Web Crawlers

HTML is short for Hypertext Markup Language and HTML documents are predominantly text-based. HTML provides the structure and format for a webpage and organizes the text, images and programs on that webpage in a meaningful way.

The next time you are using the internet and access a page, right click on the webpage and choose the option 'view page source' (or a similar sounding option). This will open a new tab in your web browser showing the HTML of the website so you can see HTML in action for yourself. You probably will not understand the majority of the HTML if you haven't studied the topic for yourself, but it is useful nonetheless to know what a HTML document looks like.

When you enter a website URL in a website browser or follow a hyperlink, your website browser requests the corresponding HTML document through the internet. The server where this HTML document is stored then receives your request, finds the relevant HTML document and sends it back to your browser, which then loads it for you to view.

As previously mentioned, HTML documents organize the information within them in standardized ways. HTML documents will have specific sections of code which label bodies of texts as titles, headers, descriptions, paragraphs and several other categories.

For example <p>This is a paragraph</p> is very basic HTML code. The <p></p> tags tells the web browser that any text within those tags should be considered a paragraph, which in this case is the text 'This is a paragraph'.

Search engines work by using software to send what is referred to as a 'spider', or more technically as A Web Crawler through HTML documents and index them within their own severs. Then when presented with a search query, search engines pass through indexed material and analyze the text and HTML to best resolve the search query.

For example, if you enter 'basketball' in to a particular search engine, that search engine will send out a web crawler through HTML documents indexed in its sever to see if the word basketball occurs in the HTML document.

It's important to note that the web crawler will only look in certain sections of the HTML document, as most of the HTML code is not useful to search through. This is why understanding the different HTML labels are important for SEO (refer to chapter 2).

If there are any matches, these will be presented as the results from the search engine query. The search engine also has various mathematical formula and algorithms to attempt to determine the importance and relevance of each matching result and thus list the webpages in a meaningful order.

For example, one of the most rudimental ways search engines originally determined importance was to measure the frequency of the word or phrase entered into the search engine bar. So if 'basketball' was the search engine query, the search engine might favor a website that has the word 'basketball' listed 10 times over a website that only has the word 'basketball' 5 times.

However, modern search engines are much more sophisticated and intricate then this fundamental method. Search engines will digest more complicated information such as where keywords appear, the relationship between them and data – such as internet traffic – to determine search engine results. So, for the query basketball, other relevant words might be 'ball', 'hoop', 'sport', 'score', 'court', 'team' and how these words are put together might influence the search engine result.

The best search engines will combine dozens, if not hundreds of different measures to calculate what webpage best matches the query presented. This produces a 'page rank', which is the order in which results are presented. Good search engines also have methods to deal with tampering and excessive manipulation (chapter 6).

To return to the frequency example, if greater frequency of keywords leads to a higher search result, this can create the temptation to simply spam a keyword a hundred or a thousand times within a webpage, with no other content, so that a certain webpage is always the first result. Such techniques were very prevalent during the early days of the web, eventually causing search engines to wise up and disregard certain results.

Nonetheless, SEO researchers and other technologically inclined individuals often deduce patterns in search engine results and therefore the nature of the algorithms behind them. As a result, large search engines like Google tend to make the names of certain algorithms and what they do public, even if they do not detail *how* they work (see chapter 3).

However, it is known that all search engines make use of keywords as well as the prevalence of backlinks to a particular website or webpage. A backlink is basically just a hyperlink; it is link back to your webpage or website, left somewhere else on the internet.

The more you delve into the details of search engine optimization, the more complicated the topic becomes. For the average business owner and more basic website, understanding every minute aspect of SEO is rather excessive; simply learning and exploiting the largest factors – such as keyword manipulation and backlinking – is enough to produce tangible results.

Organic vs. Inorganic Searches

Be aware that all the information provided is only relevant to *organic* search engine results. Most contemporary search engines also make use of *inorganic* search engine results; paid advertisements that are guaranteed to appear when certain queries are entered.

Inorganic SEO may be useful to your company or webpage, yet is not typically implied by most uses of SEO. Furthermore, inorganic SEO often requires a notable investment whereas clever SEO is often cheap or at the very least, affordable. Naturally, this organic SEO tends to more viable for most small and moderate sized businesses that may just be developing and learning about SEO.

White Hat Techniques

There are a number of official resources and guidelines that are available if you wish to research the topic of SEO further. It is in the interest of popular search engines to help websites and businesses accurately index and advertise themselves to their search engines; this increases the effectiveness of the search engine, and thus the respective company's influence.

Techniques that are promoted and embraced by search engine companies are often called 'white hat' techniques. Conversely, techniques which are strictly forbidden are termed 'black hat' techniques (chapter 6).

Other Marketing Strategies

Be conscious that there are alternative internet marketing strategies available to the informed business or website owner. Although SEO is often useful, your time might be more productive and efficient with other internet marketing techniques such as embedded advertising.

However, most of these techniques – such as social media marketing or email marketing – tend to promote and strengthen each other. As we will explore in chapter 7, most companies that are mindful of SEO also make a concerted effort with social media marketing.

Staying Up To Date

Finally, be aware that SEO is constantly changing and evolving. The algorithms that search engines employ to filter results by relevance are constantly being altered by mathematicians and computer technologists to produce better results.

Furthermore, new competitors for your website or business are always appearing and may overtake your page ranking. Additionally, internet marketers by nature are innovative and entrepreneurial; they are always finding better ways to exploit SEO and work with the system.

The point to take home here is that the world of SEO is fast and furious and you will need to keep up. As SEO evolves you will need to adapt and redouble your efforts if you wish to stay relevant. There is no guarantee that a short SEO campaign will lead to longevity in any search engine. Keep track of your page rank in various SEOs, as well as any new techniques and tricks that may arise in the future.

Also be on the watch for any changes in the algorithms that search engines use. Chapter 3 will discuss the current status of Google's known algorithms, but these algorithms are *always* being updated, and there will be many more advances in the following months and years.

In this past year alone, there were two known large scale changes to Google core algorithms (Panda 4.2 and Mobilegeddon, see chapter 3). SEO researchers have also reported two possible significant updates in February and May of 2015, although there were no official announcements.

There are hundreds of websites falling by the wayside by failing to appreciate the advances in search engine algorithms. For example, in 2011, *Demand Media*, an upcoming web-based company lost $6.4 million dollars due to the original Google Panda release. All it takes is a simple change in the search engine's programming to cause a paramount change in a company's profit.

You must stay current with the advances that SEO researchers make. Once upon a time it was considered that all keywords were valuable, yet in the last few years there has been a shift to recognizing transactional keywords as being by far the most significant (chapter 4). Similarly, backlinking is viewed differently, with more emphasis on generating few higher quality trusted back links over numerous low quality untrustworthy backlinks (chapter 5).

This book will provide you with the most up to date techniques in order to help you stay current. Nonetheless, take initiative and keep track of popular blogs and research websites such as *Search Engine Land* and *Moz* that will help keep you up to date with the most current techniques.

2

HTML, WEBSITE DESIGN AND SEO

Programming and HTML can appear overwhelming at first. There are hundreds of dozens of programming languages such as Java, JavaScript, C, C++, Python, Ruby, Pearl and more. All of these programming languages have their own syntax and conventions that need to be adhered to; to master them can take years, if not decades of study.

These programming languages are always being updated and improved, forcing programmers to stay vigilant and up to date of any changes or risk having their programs to crash.

Strictly speaking, HTML, whilst similar to a programming language, is in fact a slightly different entity. HTML lacks the capacity to perform the logical and mathematical computations that makes programming so powerful. Instead, HTML is a computer-based language of instructions and formatting, which is actually a lot simpler and straightforward. In other words, you don't need to be a computer specialist or have particularly advanced technological abilities to have a basic understanding of HTML.

Unless you are a website designer, it is unlikely that you are going to write the HTML of your website or webpage yourself. However, understanding the significance of certain HTML code is important when working with a website designer, who may or may not appreciate SEO themselves.

When working with a website designer, indicate where you want your SEO crucial text to be. Likewise, for website constructors which do most of the HTML work for you, you also have the power to manipulate your text for maximum SEO impact.

Titles

With this established, let us spend the rest of the chapter discussing the basic HTML foundations relevant to improving your SEO.

Firstly, each webpage on a website will have a title. In addition to informing people of the topic of that webpage, titles are particularly important because these are what, in most circumstances, search users will see in the search results list as the hyperlink. This hyperlink is what will direct you to the corresponding webpage. If your title is inaccurate or misleading, even if you have a high page rank, users will not take notice of your result in their search results.

In terms of HTML, titles look like:

<title> Buckingham Palace – The Place where the queen lives! </title>

The title tags, <title></title>, simply surround the text which you wish to appear; these tags are processed by your browser and do not appear in the presented page.

The particular words and terms entered into the search bar as a query will appear bolded in the search results in most search engines. You can use this search engine feature to investigate and explore the impact of your keywords.

Every webpage on your websites needs a different, unique title. Your title should accurately reflect the content of your webpage, but should also be concise. Parsimony is crucial; use keywords in your title, but only those which are most important, most focused and most impactful. Unessential, lesser keywords will simply dilute your SEO.

Description

A description is the body of text which follows the title. The description introduces the rest of the webpage with more detail than the title; however it is still only a sentence or two in length. Descriptions will usually appear under the title in the search engine results. (However, in certain instances it is possible that certain search engines may search for other text to consider when populating results.) As with titles, descriptions give search users a good impression of the purpose and content of the webpage, so being parsimonious with accurate keyword use in the description section is also necessary.

The HTML of a description appears as the following and will be directly under the title HTML:

<meta name = "description' content=" The royal family resides in Buckingham palace, alongside the royal guard and several corgis">

The structure of the meta tag is slightly different from the title tag. You don't need to be concerned with the finer details, but be aware that the text in the speech commas after '**content=**' is what will actually be seen should your description tag appear. Choose this text wisely. As with webpage titles, each description for a webpage should be different. This will increase your SEO if you have a website with multiple pages with different focuses, as most websites do.

Headings

Headings are another HTML aspect used to designate importance. Headings describe the content that follows them and help provide search engines with the structure of your webpage.

Headings have values from 1-6 depending on their importance, with lower number designating higher importance.

The HTML of headings is as follows:

<h1> The History of the British Monarchy </h1>

This HTML is pretty straight forward; the text within the <h1></h1> tags is the visible heading on your webpage. As with all other aspects of HTML text descriptions, heading accuracy, conciseness and keyword parsimony are imperative.

Anchor Text

In most well designed websites, hyperlinks are disguised; rarely do you see a full website url to click on, in order to navigate through a website. Instead, website designers often use images or appropriate text as links. To demonstrate the difference, here is a hyperlink to Google's homepage:

https://www.google.co.uk/

Here is another hyperlink to Google's homepage, this time formatted differently:

Google

The latter is more common in most websites. In HTML, text used in such a way to disguise a hyperlink is called anchor text. As your intuition is probably telling you, anchor text is extremely important for SEO.

Anchor text tells search engines what the topic of the webpage linked should be. Naturally, if the last Google link had the anchor text 'dog' you would be confused when you click upon it. Anchor text is just one of the factors search engines use when considering features such as page rank, but it is nonetheless worth your attention.

The HTML of an anchor text appears as:

<a href = "http//:www.google.com"> Google </a>

The text in speech marks after **<a href=** is the link to the desired website, and the later text before **</a>** is the actual anchor text which will appear as the link to the webpage.

As with both titles and descriptions, choose an appropriate word or phrase to be your anchor text. Avoid bad practices, such as telling people they can find Google <u>here</u> – using Google as the anchor text would be much more appropriate.

Alt Attribute

Images used in a website typically have an associated text hidden in the HTML. This text loads when the picture fails to load; perhaps due to a failure of the software required or if the page is being viewed on an older browser or system. This text is called the alt attribute.

For search engines, alt attributes perform a function similar to anchor text. Search engines can't look at pictures so they require the alt attribute to comprehend what the picture is representing. Use relevant text in your alt attribute to describe the image or the purpose of the image, but bearing in mind the importance of parsimony.

The HTML of an alt attribute looks like:

<imgsrc ="corgi.gif", alt="A picture of the queen and her corgi">

The first section, **<imgsrc ="corgi.gif"** tells the browser to load a particular image – in this case, presumably a picture of a corgi – and the second section **alt="A picture of the queen and her corgi">** describes the alt attribute; in this case the text "A picture of the queen and her corgi".

Other Considerations

There are other aspects of website design that influence SEO but are not quite covered under the topic of HTML. Namely, your website should have an intelligent structure. Most websites have numerous webpages of varying levels of importance. Well designed websites place these webpages in a logical common-sense hierarchy.

For example, continuing the British royalty motif, a good website structure may start with a home page, telling the user this website contains everything one needs to know about the royals. Then you might have a drop down section detailing all the different webpages, perhaps in this case 'History', 'Politics', 'Illuminati' and 'Lifestyle'.

Each of these sections in turn can have other webpages within that category. For example, for the history category appropriate sub pages might be 'History of Buckingham Palace' and 'Royal Family Tree'.

By placing your website within a hierarchy, you allow search engines to determine the importance and relevance of each webpage on your website. Without an appropriate hierarchy, a web crawler going through your website might consider the webpage on the history of Buckingham palace in the same regard as your home webpage.

Finally, it can be useful to research or discuss the use of various meta tags with your web designer. Meta tags are sections of HTML that control the access between the web crawler and the search engine. By labeling certain sections you can prevent them from being 'seen' by the web crawler, or prevent more specific actions – such as links being followed or bodies of texts being used – in place of descriptions.

Meta tags are useful because they give more room to include less important content. Parsimonious and clever keyword usage has been thoroughly advocated throughout this book, however if you indicate to a web crawler that certain bodies of text are not to be regarded, one can loosen up the standards slightly. Naturally you do not want to reduce the quality and focus of your webpages too much, but meta tags can be useful to compromise on certain occasions.

3

GOOGLE

Google is the goliath and leviathan of the search engine world, and thus most other search engines will base their algorithms on how Google operates. Therefore to truly master SEO, one needs to be intricately familiar with Google's search engine. Not all the algorithms and markers Google uses are widely known, however, this chapter will discuss the publicly shared algorithms Google employs.

Before delving in to the world of Google algorithms, it is important to be comfortable with what an algorithm actually *is*. Simply put, an algorithm is a problem solving procedure used in mathematics and computer science. In theory, for most tasks people want to accomplish an algorithm could be designed which, when implemented, would result in a procedure that people can follow for said task.

What makes algorithms powerful is that they are generic problem solving tools. A set of instructions may only be able to produce one result; an algorithm can produce a relevant output for a whole range of inputs. It is not necessary to appreciate all the fine details of algorithms to work with search engines, however one does need to understand that in essence, each Google algorithm is designed to solve a particular problem. By having multiple algorithms that can solve multiple smaller problems, the largest problem, page rank, can eventually be deduced.

Google Panda

Google Panda was an algorithm introduced to the Google search engine in early 2011. The purpose of this algorithm was to evaluate and categorize low-quality and undesirable websites more effectively and thus lower the page ranking of said websites. The overall result of the initial Google Panda release was that websites which contained excessive amounts of advertising plummeted in ranking. There were also reports of social media websites being ranked higher, presumably due to the fact that these websites contained very small amounts of paid advertising.

Google Panda works by essentially filtering webpages into two categories, high-quality and low-quality. Webpages filtered into the low-quality category get penalized in page rankings by a certain amount. As Google Panda works upon webpages rather than websites, it only takes a few poorly designed pages to lower an entire website's page ranking significantly.

Google has a team of human search engine testers,

who personally test search engine algorithms and who also rank search engine results on their own. This team of human searchers uses a document, produced by Google, called the *Quality Rater Guidelines* to help inform them whether a website should be considered high quality and trustworthy. The Google Panda algorithm considers elements of the Quality Rater Guidelines in order to filter the lower quality websites away from the top search engine results.

Google updates the Quality Rater Guidelines periodically and attempts to control access to the more recent drafts. Although Google endorsed versions of the Quality Rater Guidelines can be publically accessed, these guidelines tend to be censored with the juicer SEO details removed.

When viewing Google's guidelines, keep an eye out for leaks of more recent and more detailed versions. These versions tend to be flagged and removed from the internet within a couple of weeks of being leaked, but if you stay alert you may be able to obtain a draft before they disappear, giving you greater insight into how Google Panda works.

The Google released Quality Rating Guidelines document is over 40 pages, and detailed leaked versions tend to be much longer. However, the essence of the guidelines is overall consistent and rather easy to convey.

When browsing a website, if you feel like the website is attempting to be exploitative or that you wouldn't feel comfortable entering your personal information on it, then it probably wouldn't past the Quality Rating Guidelines test.

Finally, Google Panda ratings are not permanent. You can improve or worsen your page ranking with changes to your website, and as updates to Google Panda are released websites may be hit or removed from Panda moderation.

The latest update to Google Panda is Google Panda 4.2. This change to the Google Panda algorithm is being released gradually into the web.

Google Hummingbird

Google Hummingbird was an algorithm introduced in September, 2013 in order to improve Google's understanding and recognition of context. Humans have an inherent ability to infer what a word might mean from the sentence and paragraph that word is within. Likewise, we also can deduce factors such as the relative importance and emphasis of certain words from how a sentence is formulated. Using such factors, humans, in general, are much better at interpreting meaning from text compared to software, such as search engines. Google Hummingbird aimed to give search engines some of this power.

With Hummingbird released, Google now takes into account the entire phrase or sentence of a search engine query. Additionally, Google also can interpret and respond to more conversational inputs and text on webpages. For example, most people when searching for an answer to a topic or a specific piece of information, will write their search query as a 'who', 'what', 'when', 'why' or 'how' style question. E.g. - instead of simply searching 'the Queen' a user is more likely to search something such as 'how old is the queen' or 'when did the Queen become the monarch' and so on. Google Hummingbird increases the efficacy of such searches.

Hummingbird had little overt impact on how websites performed in terms of their page rank. Nonetheless, Hummingbird did emphasize 'long tailed keywords' more than previously; it just appeared that webpages already utilizing long tailed keywords and conversational text content were already receiving higher page ranks.

Long tailed keywords refer to keywords that are three or four words, or entire phrases. For example, the phrase 'wooden furniture polish' refers to a particular product by combining the meaning of all the three words used.

The term 'long tail' arises from the downwards bell curve which would result if the results of the search engine queries were plotted on a graph. Whilst particular keywords might be much more common than others, SEO researchers have discovered the majority of search engine queries are actually rare and unique entries – coined 'long tail keywords'. Therefore by ignoring long tail keywords, you actually marginalize the majority of search engine users. Learn more about long tailed keywords in chapter 4.

Google Penguin

Google Penguin is an algorithm which was introduced in April, 2012. Google Penguin aims to better detect the usage of 'black hat techniques' and webpages that break Google's terms and conditions, which is called the *Google Webmaster Guidelines*. In particular, Google Penguin aims at better recognizing and penalizing spamdexing. Black hat techniques are covered in chapter 6, but if you wish to learn more, check out the Google Webmaster Guidelines which outlines various black hat techniques to avoid (support.google.com/webmasters/answers).

The last known Google Penguin update was Penguin 3.5. The exact method Google Penguin uses is not commonly known; like much of the data and algorithms Google uses, the actual workings of

Google Penguin are shrouded in corporate secrecy.

However, it is known that Google is currently working upon a large update to Google Penguin, which will allow the algorithm to function in real time. This will allow webpages that are penalized by Google Penguin to make changes to their webpage for instantaneous effect. Currently there is a notable delay for webpages flagged for breaking the web masters guidelines to regain their standing.

Google 'Mobilegeddon'

Google's search engine contains an algorithm that provides different results for those browsing the web through a mobile phone. Mobile internet usage already exceeds internet usage from laptops and its growth will only continue to increase as smart phone usage expands their market penetration worldwide. Owing to this, it has become exceptionally important for search engines to tailor their efforts to include mobile phone users.

Naturally mobile phone screens are much smaller than laptop or desktop screens and mobile users must view and navigate webpages differently. Google has always attempted to link mobile users to 'mobile friendly' webpages, which consider mobile users and ensure that their content is accessible to a mobile audience.

However, on April 21st 2015, Google released a large update to the mobile algorithm, which many SEO researchers termed 'Mobilegeddon'. Unfortunately for SEO researchers, the intricacies of the Mobilegeddon update have yet to become publically available. No-one outside the Google company have access to its inner workings. Nonetheless the results are apparent, with data demonstrating that mobile friendly websites receive more organic internet traffic following the change.

Despite the obscurity of Mobilegeddon's inner mechanisms, you can ensure your website is mobile friendly using the *Google Developers Mobile-Friendly Test* (google.com/webmasters/tools/mobile-friendly).

Google Adwords

Google Adwords is different from the other sections discussed in this chapter. The previous sections refer to specific algorithms, yet Google Adwords is an entire system of advertising and data tracking which users can interact with. Google Adwords concerns itself primarily with inorganic search results and paid advertising options.

Regardless if one is interested in considering paid options, these inorganic results are still competitive and influenced by SEO and are therefore still useful to be aware of. Furthermore, SEO and internet advertising often go hand-in-hand – so it is important to have insight into Adwords, one of the biggest advertising productions on the web.

Google Adwords offers two different pricing schemes for its services. There are performance based pricing schemes such as pay-per-click, where the original advertiser is only charged when search engine goers click upon the link they see. The price of pay per click can vary from a fraction of a cent to over dozens of dollars (although you should anticipate lower costs for most businesses). Higher prices are generally for larger industries with long-term consumers who spend great amounts.

There are, however, pricing schemes such as cost per impression, where a flat amount is charged whenever an advertisement is presented on a webpage.

Whatever pricing option chosen, businesses still need to bid against competitors and their advertisements to appear on certain keywords. All Adwords advertisements are based upon targeting keywords, but only so many adverts can appear when certain keywords are entered. Therefore Google employs an auction-type system where businesses pay for the control over certain sets of keywords.

Fortunately, Google Adwords isn't all about bidding.

Google Adwords also formulates a quality rating of your website which uses such factors such as where your advertisement link actually leads, how relevant that webpage is, and how often people click upon the advert. Google advertisements can appear on any search engine associated with Google, such as Ask.com. Google also provides other advertising partnerships with non-search engine websites via platforms such as *AdSense*.

All advertisements thus have an 'adrank' which functions similar to a page rank; it determines where and how accessible the advert appears. Adrank is based upon the before mentioned quality ranking as well as the amount you are willing to bid. Therefore, if your advertising campaign is deemed high quality you are 'rewarded' by having to pay less and having better advertisement placement.

Google Adwords also offers tools such as the targeting of specific demographics, by ensuring that advertisements only appear on certain websites and domain names – which presumably correspond to a certain desired audience. Additionally, Google Adwords also offers a simplified service, Google Adwords *Express*, aimed at smaller businesses.

Although Google Adwords is quite a large and complex effort; Google Adwords *Express* offers a similar service, but with most of the leg work, such as keyword targeting, done automatically. For more information about how to use Google Adwords, refer to chapters 4 and 5.

Although many people learn about organic SEO in order to save time and money, sometimes it may be more economic to go for the inorganic route with paid advertising. If you are unsure about what is best for you, consult chapter 5 'SEO strategy'.

Personalized Search and Google Now

Personalized search isn't exactly a feature of Google and Google alone – most modern search engines will use personalized search to produce better results for repeat users. Nonetheless, Google uses personalized search and any SEO researcher needs to have a firm handle on personalized search basics.

When a search engine produces a personalized search (i.e. a search that is tailored to a particular user) the search engine will investigate and consider that user's internet browser cookies. Cookies are simply small pieces of data that your internet browser stores about your internet activity. Popular and frequent cookies store information such as username and password details, allowing this information to automatically appear when you re-visit a certain website (ultimately allowing you to login faster).

By taking your browser cookies into account, Google

can then adjust the page rank of webpages based on your individual preferences. For example, Google may realize you are a frequent internet shopper or that you often visit the same particular shopping website and automatically place that webpage first in your page rank results.

In addition to using browser cookies, personalized search also works by storing the internet history of individuals who are logged in to a Google service. Then, in a similar way to browser cookies, Google will formulaically adjust search engine results. Although there are many privacy controversies about search history, this issue is lessened by the fact that Google only retains data about search history for 180 days.

At first glance, personalized search may appear to be a SEO researcher's nightmare. SEO is all about recognizing patterns in how search engines operate. If each and every search is personalized to each and every user than these general patterns become less relevant to SEO. As personalized search becomes more effective, this concern does indeed become more pressing. Nonetheless, currently, it is still possible to work with personalized search and exploit how the personalized search formula works.

Most personalized searches use the following factors; country, region and social contacts. Using your IP address, a search engine will be able to determine from where you are using their service. This will allow them to interpret your query and present appropriate results.

For example, using the on-going 'Queen' theme, for most westerners the Queen will probably refer to the Queen of the British monarchy. Yet many European countries still have existing monarchies, with their own queens. Therefore if you search for the 'Queen' and you live in Denmark, the Netherlands or Liechtenstein you are likely to get some results based on the Queen in those regions.

However, location based personalization also takes into account the region which you live within. Intra-regional differences may cause search engines to rank websites with events, shops and products related to your city or town higher than generic results.

This regional personalization is especially important for businesses with a local appeal, such as restaurants or tourist-based shops. For android users, Google's search engine uses a feature called *Google Now*. Google Now aims at increasing the conversion rate of search results and the information presented to actual consumer expenditure by providing android users with more relevant local-based services.

Google Now presents 'cards' of information on a user's phone based upon a search engine query at formulaically determined appropriate times. These cards consist of useful information such as the weather forecast, news, directions and bus routes. These cards also often present information such as the highest rated shop or service nearby, and owing to this are important for regional-based businesses.

You can improve the likelihood of being recognized and recommended by Google Now in several ways. Firstly, create a Google+ account for your business. Next, have a strong social media presence on Google+, but also popular social media websites such as Facebook, Twitter and Instagram. Encourage people to leave reviews on your Google+ profile, as high ratings are particularly important for recommendations. Likewise, interact with any questions or queries presented to your Google+ or social media profiles.

Ensure you provide relevant, up-to-date contact details, address and verifications of your identity to both your Google+ profile as well as your website.

Finally, be comfortable with your HTML and the techniques introduced in chapter two. There are also many third-party websites that offer HTML-associated support, such as *Schema* (schema.org). Schema focuses on creating shared vocabulary to categorize subjects for search engines and is therefore useful when deciding what keywords to put in your HTML. Schema is in act sponsored by Google itself, so it is especially worth checking out if you are interested in this particular area.

4

KEYWORDS AND
KEYWORD RESEARCH

It should now be evident just how important keywords are to SEO. One targets their HTML and text content at just a few relevant keywords, hoping to maximize their SEO. Yet poorly chosen keywords are clearly harmful to SEO, and misguided or inaccurate keywords are even worse. It is a fine line to tread.

This chapter will address some of these challenges and give instruction on how to research and determine the best keywords for your website or webpage.

Research Unfamiliar Topics

The first and most simple method is to do a bit of research and experimentation with your own personal experience. First, become familiar with several search engines. If you live in the West you are most likely using Google as your primary search engine, nonetheless, humor other less popular search engines such as Yahoo, Bing and Ask.com. Together these search engines gather a large amount of users and should also be factored into your SEO (although Google remains more influential than the rest combined).

Next, research and learn about a topic you are not familiar with. Enter the same search queries into each search engine and consider the results. Are they the same for every website? Are there any interesting patterns you notice? Do you get the results you expect from the searches you are entering?

It is likely that, at least initially, there will be a mismatch between how important or useful you think certain queries are and the results which are presented. You haven't quite figured out the right keywords for this topic yet. Or conversely, often being naïve about a topic is one of the best ways to discover what a regular user, who is also naïve, enters when researching or looking for a particular result.

If you are attentive, you may realize that specialized search queries tend to produce very particular results. Or to paraphrase, people who search for more complicated terms or unique phrases tend to already know what they are looking for.

For example, if someone searches 'laptops' then they probably want to browse a website which will show them a range of laptops for them to consider buying. Yet if they search 'Acer 5750', they have a much higher likelihood of wanting to buy that laptop in particular, or associated parts.

This is useful to consider when thinking about your audience. The more knowledgeable and particular you anticipate your target audience to be, the more specific and precise your keywords will also be.

Research Familiar Topics

After having experimented with search engine queries with a topic you are not familiar with, start to research search engine results for the topic relating to your website or webpage. Brainstorm a list of words or phrases you consider relevant to the topic and analyze what results appear. Be systematic and organized with your investigation. Write your supposed key words down, as well as the top five or ten results. An excel spreadsheet can be useful for this type of activity.

Consider whether the results were what you anticipated. If your competitors are ranking higher than your website on a search engine, browse through their website. It may be the case that you begin to recognize clever HTML usage or a particular style or keyword use that is effective. Take note of these.

Once you have thoroughly investigated and generated a hypothesis about keyword usage and results for that particular query, actively test these ideas. Try different variations and make small alterations to your own website or webpage. If you think that one keyword is more influential than another, replace all instances of the original keyword with the latter. Then search for your website and see whether you have increased or decreased with page rank. It's possible that small immediate alterations can massively influence your SEO.

Target Transactional Based Searches

Search engine queries are predominantly categorized into three types based on intent; informational queries, navigational queries and transactional queries. Informational queries look to gather more information about a wide topic such as 'cold brewed coffee'. Navigational queries seek a particular, singular result – a webpage or company such as 'Reddit' or 'Walmart'. Transactional queries are those which seek a method to complete a desired action – such as buying a product.

The important point here is knowing what type of search engine query to target: transactional queries.

Navigational queries tend to be fruitless to target if you are not the business or entity being searched for (as the search engine user will ignore other results because they already know what they are looking for). Informational queries cover such a vast range of results and also tend to be pointless to attempt to monetize.

If someone searches 'cold brewed coffee', for example, it is hard to deduce in what way this internet activity could result in a profit somewhere. The searcher may just want to know what cold brewed coffee is or how to make it. Even if they are looking for a product, the internet is still too wide; are they looking for coffee grind, a restaurant or café that serves cold brew coffee or for equipment such as a French press?

Owing to this, targeting transactional search queries is the most viable option. Targeting transactional queries will produce better conversion rates between searches and actual expenditure.

To target transactional queries, focus on commercial-based keywords such as 'buy', 'discount', 'order', 'delivery'. These words communicate the searcher already wants to make a purchase and is just looking for a means to do so. If you have a special angle, such as 'free delivery', make sure this is especially emphasized.

Likewise, also focus upon commercial language specifically related to your product such as 'cheap' or 'high range'. For certain businesses, for example a computer based businesses, more advanced language such as 'high performance' or 'good graphics' might be targetable transactional keywords too.

Use Google Adword Tools

As part of its Adwords service, Google also offers a keyword planner. This keyword planner provides data showing how often certain keywords are used, but it also suggests certain keywords that can be useful for you as well. By employing both of these services, you can identify new keyword combinations that have a high search rate. Bearing in mind the previous strategy tip, focus on keyword combinations that fall within the transactional category and deliver commercial intent.

Additionally, keyword planner shows the history of keyword searches. This is useful for discovering trends in search patterns based on real world events. For example, for big companies such as Apple or Samsung, search engine queries related to these companies will probably spike when they release a large, new product.

Alternatively, events such as widely spread news stories or viral internet hashtags can influence search engine query popularity. Keyword usage even varies massively by obvious changes, such as the progression of seasons. Winter clothing and Christmas presents are bound to be less popular during the middle of June.

If you can associate an increase of keywords with a particular event, this gives you the opportunity to be mindful of when a similar event might occur. Therefore you can tactfully alter your keywords and change your webpage content based on anticipated events that influence keyword usage.

In addition to Adword tools, *Google Trends* (google.com/trends) is a good source of information about which topics are currently popular, or have been in the past.

Adwords tools also provides information about the competition and market share for keywords. It is likely that keywords with high competition reflect most relevant transactional based queries for a given sector. Nonetheless, if you can find an area or niche where a transactional based keyword search is popular but where competition is low, ensure you fully exploit and capitalize on that keyword or keyword combination.

Finally, also work with *Google Analytics* (google.com/analytics). Google Analytics provides information such as the conversion rate between a keyword entry and an actual purchase, or data such as the amount of time someone spent browsing your website. Due to a variety of external factors, it may be the case that even popular transactional keywords have low conversion rates. If this is the case then obviously abandon them and look for keywords with higher conversation rates.

5

SEO STRATEGY AND ROI

The most important stage for the serious SEO user is to calculate whether it is more efficient to concentrate their main efforts on SEO, or spend money and attention on different ventures - such as pay per click advertising. All smart business owners will be constantly evaluating their return on investment (ROI).

The first stage in working out ROI is to investigate how much money your website is making from search engine page results (SERP's) currently. This requires using third-party resources, such as Google Analytics, to measure the amount of organic traffic your website receives in a given time frame. In this example, let's imagine that your webpage generates approximately 10,000 webpage views per month.

Next, you need to identify the conversion rate of these web views; the amount of people who are actually buying a product, service or meaningfully engaging in your website – such as subscribing to an email list. In this scenario, let us envision a conversion rate of 5%. With 10,000 people visiting your website every month at a conversion rate of 5%, this will result in 500 people purchasing or engaging with your website.

Next, determine the average purchase amount on your website and how much profit this will generate you. In this example, let's suppose that the average purchase results in $5 of profit. Using the previous value of 500 people visiting your website, we can deduce that $5 x 500 is $2500. Therefore, organic results will produce approximately $2500 in profit for the website.

The $2500 estimate gives a value to work with when considering the ROI for any investments made towards SEO. Considerations could include money spent on third-party analytics and websites, or the approximate monetary value of your time focused in this area.

Let's suppose a budget of $3000 for your SEO campaign. Using the anticipated conversion rate of 5% of your internet traffic to purchasing customers and an average profit of $5, we can calculate how many more page views you will need for SEO to become profitable. $3000 equates to 600 purchases. As only 5% of your internet traffic is purchasing, you need 20 times that amount of page views to generate that profit, or an additional 18,000 views.

We now have an estimate of 18,000 additional views as the impact that our SEO campaign needs to make for us to break even. With this number, using data on the page views that highly ranked SERP's receive as well as considering the amount of traffic that that particular keywords generates, we can determine whether 18,000 extra views is feasible.

Let's suppose we know that the first result of a keyword on Google receives 50% of all traffic, then the second result receives 20% and the next three receive 10% each. You need to anticipate what position your SEO campaign will place you. Let's be optimistic and say we are aiming for second place on the search results of 20% of traffic.

We now need to know the amount of people searching for that keyword or keyword combination. Let us say our keyword being searched for is 'Russian Dictionary' which receives 50,000 searches every month. By shooting for second place, we are aiming to receive 20% of the 50,000 Russian dictionary searchers, so an additional 10,000 people.

We need to repeat the process of calculating anticipated page views for every keyword we are targeting. After this, we can total our anticipated extra page views and determine whether it exceeds our 18,000 required views to see whether our SEO campaign is anticipated to be profitable.

If we choose to proceed with an actual SEO campaign, we can measure the increase in page views our website receives, the conversion rate of these views and the profit gathered to compare our actual ROI to our anticipated ROI.

All the information you require should be obtainable either from *Google Analytics*, *Google Keyword Planner* and a little investigation on the web. A study from 2013, for example, claims that the first result on Google receives 33% of internet traffic and the second receives 17.6%, third place at 11.4% and so on. Search carefully!

Recent Tips and Tricks

> Avoid Personalized Search

Personalized search is persistent and ubiquitous. If researching for purposes of SEO, any results you gather may be tainted by your own personalized search and may not reflect the results other searchers see. As Google stores the internet history of computers based upon their IP, you cannot avoid personalized search simply by deleting your history and removing internet cookies. Even if you access another computer, away from your IP, you are likely to run into personalized search again, this time the personalized search of that computer user.

To avoid and control the influence of personalized search, use third party tools such as *Rank Tracker* (link-assistant.com/rank-tracker) which can filter away personalized search results by manipulating your IP address.

> Generate Trusted Backlinking

As previously mentioned, Google also considers aspects such as authority and trust when determining page rank. If a website is regarded to be a credible, reliable source of information for a particular topic, then it will receive a high page rank whenever that topic is being searched for.

Likewise, if a website is trusted with sensitive information then search engines will naturally promote it over its less credible, less trusted competitors. Inbound links are considered the most important factor in your Google page ranking, so getting them correct is essential.

Use the credibility and authority of other websites to your advantage by backlinking your website via these trusted websites. A backlink through a credible website will mean much more than a backlink through a website that is not trusted, or even penalized. Communicate and ask whether you can guest blog or guest feature your website or business with other reputable websites. Networking is a powerful tool – sometimes all you need is the confidence to ask.

Additionally, you can also use third-party resources such as *Impactana*. Impactana will allow you to search keywords and discover websites that have the highest amount of content shared across social media, relevant to those keywords.

6

BLACK HAT TECHNIQUES

All of the previous chapters have instructed on how to maximize SEO using 'white hat' techniques. These techniques are actively encouraged and supported by search engines and are considered mutually beneficial. Nonetheless, 'black hat' techniques exist, and the topic of SEO isn't complete without discussing some of the more precarious options.

Firstly, you need to be aware of black hat techniques so you don't end accidently use them. For example, we have discussed keywords thoroughly throughout this guide. Although it is no longer effective, some people fall prey to the temptation of simply spamming their website with repeated keywords ('spamdexing').

This can range from bad practice to clear and overt manipulation, such as when a keyword is just repeated say 100 times in a row (often hidden in the HTML previously mentioned in chapter 2, in order to not affect user experience). If you are ignorant of spamdexing, you may just innocently end up close to doing it by using keywords perhaps a little too frequently. Knowing about spamdexing keeps you safe and allows you to re-consider whether your keyword frequency is too high.

Additionally, it is important to be familiar with black hat techniques in case your website comes under attack. It is not unheard of for business competitors to resort to less virtuous means and hack their counterpart's websites, filling them with black hat SEO techniques. The result, if not responded to, is that a website can be unfairly blacklisted and thus removed from search engine competition.

In addition to hacks, user spam and various other types of third-party activity can appear to be black hat techniques to search engines, also resulting in black listing.

Depending on your sensibilities, you may or may not be interested in black hat techniques for your personal use. As a general rule of thumb, your standard long-term SEO strategy will want to use white hat techniques and white-hat techniques only.

Some short-term businesses looking for rapid profits will willingly embrace black hat techniques to garner the best SEO in the shortest amount of time. This may result in their websites becoming blacklisted, however if those short-term profits are sufficient, some businesses are happy to make the trade.

Not all black hat techniques are forbidden by law.

Black hat techniques are against the terms of service of search engines, but most black hat techniques only result in said search engines penalizing black hat users. Black hat techniques also vary in how they are morally regarded; some techniques are designed to steal the profit or attention from other websites, other merely annoy the search engines.

Black hat techniques may not make the search engines happy, but your interests and the interests of these engines may not always align. If you want to go down the route of black hat SEO techniques, you need to thoroughly understand all the advantages and disadvantages of what you are doing.

In most cases the decision to stick to white hat techniques is more profitable, yet it would be dishonest to convey that no-one thinks otherwise. Although it is strongly recommended sticking with white hat SEO techniques, it is ultimately up to you to choose your own course of action once you are familiar with all the facts.

Hidden Text

This black hat technique is very simple. Text is formatted via CSS, a computer language that deals with the more stylistic elements of HTML, to appear invisible. This invisibility is often as basic as having white text appear on a white background so the user cannot see such said text unless they attempt to highlight it. Additionally, having text appear so small that it is practically unseen or any other type of manipulation designed to prevent users from actually reading the text is considered a type of hidden text.

There are innocent uses of hidden text in websites, such as spoiler prevention when talking about stories, books, films and T.V. However, hidden text can also be used intentionally to include text patterns that appeal to search engines, but which do not affect user experience. Naturally this irritates search engines as search engines try to produce the best results according to user experience.

Furthermore, hidden text can also be used to hide links. This can increase the amount of backlinking towards a particular website increasing the SEO, without genuinely incorporating these links in a meaningful way. This will also aggravate search engines.

Spam Ping

Websites can release messages to search engines and other corners of the web, signaling that new content to the website has been added. This is a healthy and expected function of most websites and it provides an opportunity for search engines to re-evaluate their prominence. One would infer that if a website is continually receiving fresh updates, then this website it likely in a stage of growth and improvement. At the very least, it suggests a certain level of effort.

However, it is possible to manipulate these messages and automate them to occur more frequently then the release of new content. In fact, many black hat users use software to suggest that new content is being produced every couple of minutes, or even quicker. Obviously if this is not true, search engines will not be happy with such blatant manipulations.

Website Copying

This is exactly what it sounds like; copying the content from another website. There is nothing wrong with quoting a different website and responsibly citing and linking to said website. However when large bodies of text or other content is copied, without links, then it starts to be considered a problem. It also goes without saying that creating a direct identical copy of another website will not do you any favors either.

Bait and Switch

This technique refers to creating a website or webpage that is well SEO optimized, but then dramatically changing the content of said webpage. This is considered to be particularly deceitful when the content is changed to be completely irrelevant to the original search topic.

Making updates and improvements to a website is of course a part of basic website maintenance, but ensure that the original vision or intent of the website is still preserved throughout these changes. It is when websites are completely redrawn and repurposed overnight that they are considered to have been baited and switched.

Cloaking

Cloaking is a technique that essentially tricks the search engines into believing that they are accessing one website when they are in fact accessing a different one. A false page is designed to appeal to the web crawlers, who categorize the page in the way the HTML implies. However, for human users, a second genuine page is presented with content that is entirely unrelated to the false page. The result is that the second page is given the page rank that should correspond to the first.

The false page is generally designed in a way that is predicted or known to generate a high page rank and a lot of internet views. The genuine page, the one that the user experiences, tends to be less naturally popular. The overall result is that traffic is generated for the unpopular page which it otherwise wouldn't receive.

Cloaking is caused by IP manipulation.

Gateway Pages

A gateway page is a webpage whose primary purpose is to re-direct internet views elsewhere. There is nothing inherently wrong or discouraged about gateway pages. However, black hat SEO can involve making gateway pages use certain exploitative techniques – such as keyword spamming and hidden text – to generate large amounts of internet traffic.

These gateway pages then re-direct the internet traffic to an unrelated website. Often this re-direction is forced through programming, such as JavaScript, so that viewers of the gateway page have no choice but to end up on the unintended page.

Naturally search engines do not want to lead users to websites they have no actual interest in. Therefore, when considering creating a gateway page, ensure that the gateway contains information that is relevant to your website and that your links are appropriate. Never force your user to go to another page if they don't want to; make sure linking is consensual.

Blog Link Spam

If you ever frequent blogs on Tumblr, Wordpress or even the comments section of online news sources, you will see blog link spam all the time. Blog link spam is exactly what it sounds like; individuals leave links in the comments section of blogs and other websites in order to increase the backlinking of a particular website.

There is nothing wrong with posting a related or associated link when it is relevant to the topic of discussion or other comments on the blog, however when completely random links are posted as comments on blogs it is considered to be blog link spam.

URL Hijacking

This practice involves taking advantage of existing websites that already have a high page ranking by creating URL's and domain names that are extremely similar to existing popular domains in order to gain traffic from these websites.

For example, Reddit is a popular website, accessed via the URL **www.reddit.com**. If someone were to register a website called www.redd**d**it.com, then this would be taken by the search engines in bad faith; it is a clear attempt to gain traffic from people misspelling the intended domain. This is considered especially deceitful when the hijacked website is designed to confuse or bewilder people trying to access the intended website by having it designed in the same way or providing similar content.

7

SOCIAL MEDIA AND ONLINE CONTENT

Masterful HTML, using keywords or avoiding black hat techniques can only take one so far. The most obvious and important aspect of raking in the rankings of a search engine is for your content to be *good*.

The information presented should be current, high quality content and provide *value* to people viewing it. Naturally, the website itself should be aesthetically pleasing - looking fresh and new. The text needs to be grammatically correct and free of spelling errors. The website should have a good overall flow. It should be interactive and engaging and needs to be able to attract and *keep* the attention of those with short attention spans.

Likewise, no notable SEO effort is complete without also considering social media influences. All search engines will consider the amount of internet traffic a website or webpage receives when determining page rank. Even if you have the best website in the world, if only 10 people view that page per year, the search engine will infer that it is irrelevant.

No SEO is complete without quality content

interconnected with various social media platforms. By advertising and creating content on social media websites, one can massively increase the amount of traffic directed to their website, indirectly increasing SEO.

This chapter will discuss the various methods on how to optimize content to increase internet traffic and therefore improve SEO.

Images and Video Frequency

One way to increase your website's attractiveness and ability to catch people's attention is to focus on image and video based content. Images are easier to digest and process than large amounts of text and can often create a more immediate, impactful impression on the browser. Likewise, videos require less effort for the viewer to passively watch and can be formatted to have a fast pace and flow, keeping low attention spans engaged with your content.

Keyword Creation

Social media campaigns are particularly effective for keyword creation and manipulation, although it is possible to create your own phrases via your website. Viral campaigns such as the 'IceBucketChallenge' (where individuals dump a bucket of ice cold water on themselves to raise money for charity) or 'WhyIStayed' (a phrase raising awareness for domestic abuse) capitalized on words and phrases that were otherwise unpopular.

What is great about these created keywords, or keyword combinations, is that they have no inherent initial competition for traffic or search results, unlike most other pre-existing keywords. However, they may have less transactional value than other keywords; use them primarily to generate traffic, rather then your main focus.

Interaction

Ensure the content produced on your various social media platforms provides lots of opportunity for interaction. Human beings are social creatures; we naturally seek positive attention and reassurance from others. Create content with explicit questions, asking what your social media followers think or feel, or provide room for discussion within your comments section. People love this, especially if you take the time to respond – however briefly – to a few posts.

Also take advantage of other forms of social interaction. One popular technique is to use the like and share functions of websites as a kind of voting tool. Ask your viewers to compare two different products or images and 'like' their preferred choice. This type of activity can be useful for market research purposes, but even if the results are irrelevant people are engaged by the interaction your website offers.

Social Media Promotions

Most social media websites offer specific tools for businesses using their platform. These tools allow businesses to garner popularity, for a price. For example, social media accounts offer small rewards for following or subscribing to particular profile pages. This is an easy way to rapidly gain a large amount of followers for relatively little effort.

Rewards can take the form of discount codes or special offers only redeemable through certain type of social media interaction. Rewards are even more powerful if you integrate them with part of a loyalty scheme to encourage return service.

Follow and Share Other Social Media Posts

Another easy technique to develop social media popularity is to follow and share the content of other businesses and users. By sharing content from other users, people who are following the producer of the content that you share will also see your post. This is an efficient way to be seen by more people without going to great effort. This technique also promotes sociability and interaction. Highlighting a relevant post made by one of your followers is a great way to demonstrate that you are paying attention to what people are writing and positing about you.

Furthermore, following and sharing content is a useful way to ensure that relevant content is always prevalent from your social media accounts, without necessarily having to create that content yourself. People want to be entertained and engaged by your social media account, but forwarding interesting and engaging content produced by others is often good enough.

Schedule Content

Schedule your posts and provide content regularly. If you only post once a month, you will not gain many followers and people who have previously followed you or frequented your website will likely cease to due to a lack of activity. Although the scheduling and pacing of your content delivery will obviously depend on the platform you are using as well as the size of your company, aim for a post at least once per day.

At the minimum, make a post 2-3 times per week, just

to keep some presence on social media. If you cannot manage this relatively small amount of maintenance/social media presence, then re-evaluate whether you have the time to spend on social media activity at all. This may negatively impact your overall SEO maximization, but consider your limitations regardless.

For greater expansion on the powerful impact and interconnectedness social media plays with SEO and it's important role in promoting a website or brand, see *Social Media Domination: Master Social Media Marketing Strategies with Facebook, Twitter, YouTube, Instagram and LinkedIn* by Kenneth Lewis.

Prioritize Most Relevant Information

When humans share information, whether it be in a book or presentation, we present the majority of the relevant details at the beginning. Both humans and web crawlers will prioritize the content you present right away over the content you present later.

People tend to read the first few sentences and paragraphs first, and if they are not immediately intrigued or interested, they will simply abandon and exit your website. On this principle, web crawlers recognize that the most attention-grabbing details of your website need to be at the start of the webpages.

Describe Hidden Media Content

In addition to providing content people are interested in, ensure your content is also accessible by search engines. Certain types of media may not be recognized by search engine web crawlers and thus will not influence your page ranking.

For example, animated sequences using programming software such as JavaScript will not be considered by search engines. You may have taken great effort to ensure a high frequency of keywords in video or image content on your website, yet search engines do not appreciate this.

Therefore, to optimize your content for SEO, use images, videos and animations to explain concepts and gather interest but augment these media with short, keyword-dense descriptions. Your descriptions only need to be one, two or three sentences long to explain the content of the video or animation. This will influence SEO results without burdening your website with excess text.

Prioritize Accessible Content

Both web crawlers from search engines and your human audience need to be able to access your content to appreciate it. However, certain website designs and content displays will prevent your content from being accessible. For example, web crawlers will not be able to access content locked behind a login screen, and therefore neither will the majority of your web traffic.

Consider how your user is supposed to find content on your website. If they need to do something relatively complex, then it is probable that a web crawler may also struggle to find this content. In both cases, the result is that content is less accessible and less influential for SEO.

To illustrate – some websites have a structure where the user is required to answer a questionnaire or survey in order to be re-directed to another page of results. Horoscope or personality test websites that need information such as one's date of birth or star sign to produce a personal profile are good examples of these. Many people simply won't bother to enter such information, and web crawlers won't either. Ensure your important SEO relevant content is accessible before these restraints.

CONCLUSION

Thank you again for reading.

I trust this book was able to help you master the essentials of search engine optimization.

As with any aspect of life that results in profit, search engine optimization is a fiercely competitive discipline. By maximizing your SEO you are not just improving your own page rank and level of internet traffic, you are also indirectly reducing the traffic and rank of your competitors. However, most of your peers will be equally aggressive in their tactics to earn the top listing of a search result to ensure that their business is the one that succeeds.

Owing to this, it is crucial to genuinely understand how search engines work and the steps needed to be taken to optimize a website or webpage. This comprehensive guide has provided all the information and tools necessary for you to maximize your SEO and gain the edge over your competition.

You are now familiar with how search engines interact with the HTML of a website by sending our web crawlers. We discussed the complexity and nuances of algorithms, and the various calculations that search engines use to rank webpages in terms of importance and prominence. We identified the most influential of these factors, such as appropriate usage of keywords and backlinking.

We explored the aspects of HTML that are vital to how search engines prioritize websites. You are now familiar with titles, headers, descriptions, anchor text and alt attributes, and how these features appear. Advice was also offered on the significance of website hierarchy and meta tags that can control the all-important web crawlers.

We cemented your SEO expertise by methodically going through the process of researching keywords. You learned how to systematically and logically discover keywords and how you and your competitors are using them. You are now acquainted with external resources, such as Google keyword planner, which can augment your SEO efforts by providing various useful data and statistics.

The fifth chapter explored the process of determining the ROI of your anticipated SEO campaign and how to calculate whether SEO is valuable to your business and webpage.

We also discussed what *not* to do. We identified various 'black hat' techniques, which are expressly forbidden by search engines. With your knowledge, you can now avoid ignorantly stumbling into black hat territory and recognize if your website is under a black hat attack.

Finally, we explored how to optimize the content on your website, webpage and social media accounts. You learned about variables such as accessibility, scheduling, interaction and prioritization. There is now no longer an excuse for low quality, SEO unfriendly content.

Will all the strategies and techniques we have covered, you are now equipped to gain the SEO edge over your competitors and ensure that *your* website and business is the one that succeeds. I wish you the best of luck.

SHARE YOUR EXPERIENCE

Finally, if you enjoyed or benefited from this book, then I would like to ask you for a favor:

Would you be kind enough to leave your feedback in a review for this book on Amazon?

It would be greatly appreciated!

Visit <u>Amazon.com</u> and search 'SEO Kenneth Lewis' to be brought to the book's page in which you can leave your feedback.

Thank you, and best of luck on bringing your business to the next level.

BONUS EXCERPT

FACEBOOK MARKETING:
How to Use Facebook for Effective Internet
Marketing and Social Media Success

Facebook is a colossal entity with almost 1 billion daily users interacting with each other and checking their newsfeed for updates about the world. With so many people choosing to access Facebook every day, it is no wonder that it has become one of the greatest marketing assets of this decade.

Facebook actively encourages advertisement efforts on their website and other business relations, providing an abundance of tools and systems for both small and large businesses. However, trying to learn how to market through Facebook poses a steep learning curve. Although a few tips and tricks from tried and tested internet marketing guides are applicable, Facebook needs to be tackled as its own creature, with its own rules.

You need to thoroughly understand how Facebook works on a very fundamental level. This includes topics such as how Facebook determines what content is presented through the newsfeed and the underlying concept of the 'reach' and of organic content.

Your knowledge must also extend to the labyrinthine system of paid advertising and marketing. You need to appreciate the different between a boosted post, a paid advertisement and all the different decisions you should have to make, should you choose to employ either. It is also critical to know how the auction and bidding systems work; the underlying mechanism which determines the cost and charges associated with advertising on Facebook.

This, however, doesn't even cover the tip of the iceberg. You also need to be intimate with the different Facebook business objective goals and the different audiences you can target via all the options Facebook provides. There are the various pricing schemes you can chose, say as pay-per-click, pay-per-impression and optimized pay-per-click that you cannot market without. Additionally, you need to understand the three-part campaign structure of Facebook advertising and the tools offered to manage advertising, such as the power editor.

With these fundamentals covered in the initial chapter, you can then begin to stretch your marketing muscles with Facebook Insights, which presents an entire world of marketing information for you to analyze. If you want to know how many more people liked your content in the past 24 hours, or what your potential reach could be, Facebook Insights is going to be your best friend. Even if you remain mere associates, you need to appreciate Facebook Insights for what the feedback and power it offers you to refine and improve your marketing efforts.

With Facebook Insights now firmly understood, you can start to really bring your marketing tactics to the next level with more advanced strategies. If you are naïve about dark posting or if you think pixels are just to do with your screen resolution, then the strategies within this book will give you an enlightening wake-up call. Learn how to target niche audiences, improve conversions, create custom audiences and re-target missed buyers with the sophisticated and complex opportunities Facebook presents.

With your marketing expertise now reaching intimidating levels, you will then be presented with all the various resources that you can utilize to give yourself the Facebook marketing edge. Find out where you can access Facebook's free 34 part marketing e-learning course, or where you should be waiting to hear the latest Facebook news and updates.

With your Facebook mastery established, you must be prudent to stay on top of the game by keeping up to date with all the changes and updates Facebook is developing for release in the near future. Facebook puts light itself to shame with just how fast it rushes ahead.

If you simply sit on the knowledge of established techniques without taking the initiative to keep your knowledge fresh, then you will soon find yourself a Facebook novice once more. Learn about highly anticipated changes, such as Facebook Reactions, Facebook Immersive ads and Facebook Connectivity - changes that may shake the foundations of the current Facebook marketing platform we know today.

Chapter 1: Facebook Organic Reach

Originally, all content a user posted on Facebook would be seen by their followers on their news feeds. However, as Facebook became more popular and the average user subscribed to more content, Facebook implemented a system to filter and restrict the amount of content users see. Now, only a portion of content gets seen by followers, which prevents users from feeling overwhelmed as well as protect them viewing from diluted, poor content – or rather content that they simply will not be interested in. This system is called 'Facebook Reach' and refers to how far and how much penetration (i.e reach) your Facebook content achieves.

Facebook reach deals with 'organic' content. Organic refers to content that is naturally filtered through search engine and social media engines. This organic content is then ranked and filtered according to its quality, and thus generates a certain amount of exposure or traffic based on the ranking it receives.

Although most marketers will also employ Facebook Boost and Facebook Paid Advertising, Facebook Reach is where every internet marketer will want to start. If you learn to play the game and abide by the rules, you can still ensure a high amount of your organic content reaches your desired audience. Furthermore, Facebook Reach is free and is a great way for internet marketers to test the shallow waters before they dive in to the deep end.

Facebook Reach uses an algorithm to filter content and decide whether that content is worth your follower's time. The original algorithm, called 'Edgerank' uses three factors (affinity, edge weight and time decay).

Affinity, Weight and Time Decay

Affinity refers to how well two users are known to each other, and how interconnected their lives are. If two users frequently interact across Facebook, frequently tag each other or belong to many of the same groups and share many of the same friends, than these users will have high affinity. Affinity takes into account clicking on user content, liking, commenting, tagging, sharing and friend-ing as measures of connectedness.

It is important to note that affinity is asymmetrical; user A can have a high affinity towards user B without user B having high affinity towards user A.

Additionally, each action you perform on Facebook has a different 'edge weight'. Simply put, certain actions are considered more important and more telling than others. It is easy and non-committal to like or share content. Commenting however, implies a closer relationship between two users. At the very least, it signals more effort. Owing to this, commenting has a higher edge weight than liking and will be more influential in Facebook Edgerank.

To read the rest of *Facebook Marketing*, visit Amazon.com and search 'Facebook Kenneth Lewis'.

OTHER WORKS BY KENNETH LEWIS

Facebook Marketing: The 25 Best Strategies on Using Facebook for Advertising, Business and Making Money Online

Social Media Domination: Social Media Marketing Strategies with Facebook, Twitter, YouTube, Instagram and LinkedIn

A Beginner's Guide to Internet Marketing: 17 Proven Online Marketing Strategies to Make Money Online

Passive Income: Make Money Online and Achieve Financial Freedom – How to Make $500 - $12K with Only $50

The Procrastination Cure: 7 Simple Strategies to Overcome Procrastination, Increase Productivity and Develop Time Management Strategies for Life

Interview and Get Any Job You Want: Employment Techniques and How to Answer Toughest Interview Questions

All books are available in e-book and audio-book format, and many are also available in paperback as well. Visit Amazon.com to view available editions.

ABOUT THE AUTHOR

For over thirty years Kenneth has been active in the business and marketing force, working for various companies as well as pursuing his own independent projects. He has most recently began publishing introductory books on internet marketing and other various aspects of social media as a way to share his passion and interests with those who are new to these domains.

His books aim to be practical, easy to understand and follow. His books also serve as reference guides to those who are already somewhat familiar with the online marketing sector.

In his spare time, Kenneth enjoys golfing, fishing, and spending time with his family at their lake house. Kenneth is also an avid cook and enjoys experimenting with different recipes.